# THE KENDO MIND:
## A Guide to Grading Successfully

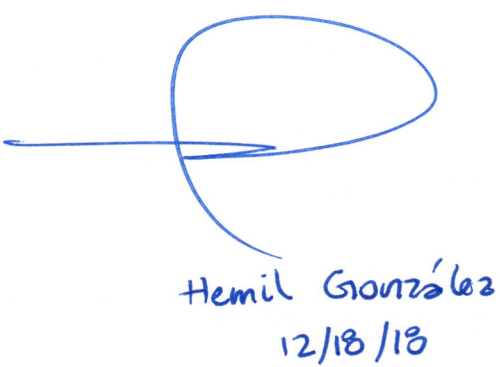

Shigematsu Kimiaki
(Kendo Kyoshi 8-dan)

©Bunkasha International Corporation
All rights reserved by Bunkasha International Corporation.
No part of this book may be used or reproduced without written permission, except for brief quotations in critical publications or reviews.

First edition published in June, 2016
Bunkasha International Corporation
2498-8 Oyumicho Chuo-ku Chiba-shi Chiba, Japan

Written by Shigematsu Kimiaki
Translated by Yamaguchi Remi
Editorial supervision by Alexander Bennett, Michael Ishimatsu-Prime
Design and Layout by Bunkasha International Corporation

*The joy of kendo is not found in striking one's opponent. It is found in the complex and multifaceted process leading up to the execution of a technique.*

# CONTENTS

**Preface** .............................................. 7

## CHAPTER 1
### *"Strike in a way that will leave an impression on the judges..."*

1. Why we need examinations ...................... 9
2. It's not so much the strike, but the *seme-ai* that counts ...................... 10
3. Who will you come up against?................. 11
4. Tidy appearance and proper *reihō*............. 12
5. *Sonkyo* is crucial for an effective strike........... 14
6. Elements of *datotsu* ........................... 16
7. Your greatest weapon is your spirit ............. 34
8. Patience after the strike ....................... 36
9. Keeping it together at the venue ............... 37
10. *Keiko* after the grading........................ 38

## CHAPTER 2
### *Cultivating your own kendo philosophy*

1. *Kirikaeshi* and *uchikomi* foster strength . . . . . . . . . . 41
2. "Two-faced" *keiko* . . . . . . . . . . . . . . . . . . . . . . . . . . . . . 44
3. The right attitude. . . . . . . . . . . . . . . . . . . . . . . . . . . . . . 45
4. Forging *ki* . . . . . . . . . . . . . . . . . . . . . . . . . . . . . . . . . . . 49
5. Consider "*kyojitsu*" . . . . . . . . . . . . . . . . . . . . . . . . . . . . 51
6. Does your kendo match your *dan*? . . . . . . . . . . . . . . 54
7. Acknowledging insufficient strikes. . . . . . . . . . . . . . . 55
8. Seek and learn . . . . . . . . . . . . . . . . . . . . . . . . . . . . . . . . 56
9. Solitary *keiko* . . . . . . . . . . . . . . . . . . . . . . . . . . . . . . . . 57
10. Discipline your mind in everyday life . . . . . . . . . . . 60
11. The teaching of *shu-ha-ri*. . . . . . . . . . . . . . . . . . . . . . . 61
12. Instructor qualities . . . . . . . . . . . . . . . . . . . . . . . . . . . . 63
13. Is your instruction appreciated?. . . . . . . . . . . . . . . . . 65
14. Kendo is about developing willpower. . . . . . . . . . . . 68
15. *Keiko* alone is not enough . . . . . . . . . . . . . . . . . . . . . . 70

**Conclusion** . . . . . . . . . . . . . . . . . . . . . . . . . . . . . . . . . . . . . . 72

**The Keiko Mindset** . . . . . . . . . . . . . . . . . . . . . . . . . . . . . . 73

# PREFACE

Those who study kendo regard promotion examinations and matches as vehicles for cultivating self-discipline. Preparing to take a grading is especially motivating compared to regular training. It is, however, also a tremendous disappointment when you fail. There are those who manage to pass each examination without ever failing, and others who reach an impasse. So, what is the difference between these two groups? If you can figure this out, even just a little, you are one step closer to finding success.

There are many things needed for success in an examination, not least of which is impressing the judges with resonating strikes. There is no way to achieve your goal without knowing how to accomplish this. The content of this book is based on lessons I learned from my sensei, my personal experiences in the dojo, and what I read in books and instruction manuals along the way. I hope that you will find the information in this small volume useful reference material as you tread down the path of kendo.

## CHAPTER 1

## *"Strike in a way that will leave an impression on the judges…"*

## 1. Why we need examinations

The "Concept of Kendo", formulated by the All Japan Kendo Federation in 1975, determines that kendo should "discipline the human character through the application of the principles of the sword", and its purpose is to nurture kendo practitioners with high moral standards.

In the "Concept of Kendo", there is no mention of the importance of attaining a higher rank or winning matches. How would you respond to someone who asks you why you will take an examination? Many people do not have a clear answer for this. My reply would be, "To have my skills and understanding of kendo principles evaluated, so that I know what I need to work on next."

Kendo training consists of constant repetition, and you cannot acquire the skills overnight. Only through continuing to train honestly and with conviction will your efforts eventually bear fruit. Examinations provide us with tangible milestones along the way.

## 2. It's not so much the strike, but the *seme-ai* that counts

A grading is an occasion where you present your kendo philosophy to experts who assess whether or not you are on the right track. What then, is your "kendo philosophy"? It is your mental attitude in training, and the way in which acknowledge and express the culture of kendo. Furthermore, one's kendo philosophy is appraised on the extent to which it is based on the "Concept of Kendo". One of the effective ways for testing the effectiveness of your *keiko* is to compete in matches. Nevertheless, there will come a time in which you must decide how result-oriented you want to be, and how much you intend to abide by the "Concept of Kendo" in the quest for self-development.

As the examination day approaches, your mental attitude at training will become more focussed. The desire to pass a looming exam is always a strong motivator to keep your kendo honest. It is more important, however, to always do your absolute best during daily trainings irrespective of whether there is an examination or not.

Let us consider the examination itself from here. You may think it is just a matter of scoring as many successful points as possible on your opponents. Effective strikes are important, but mental factors such as spirit and *seme* are more pivotal as evaluation criteria. The higher the grade, the more it is expected that you show your strikes are intentional, and not just random or lucky hits. Keep in mind that successfully striking your opponent does not guarantee a pass. At gradings for high-ranking kendoka, strikes are the culmination of first overcoming the opponent psychologically, or defeating them before the strike. It is not a hitting competition. An examination is about *seme*—the process of applying pressure and controlling the opposition.

If you complain that you weren't passed even though you decimated your opponent, it is an indication that your kendo outlook is immature and underdeveloped.

## 3. Who will you come up against?

Your opponents will be roughly the same age and rank; in other words, kenshi of a parable skill level who meet the requirements to take the examination. In the limited time given, judges will evaluate your overall performance. This includes your attire, *reihō* (etiquette), posture, *maai* (distance and timing), *seme* (applying pressure to create openings), striking opportunities, *zanshin* (post-strike physical and psychological alertness), and so forth. Examinees are under pressure to demonstrate their technical ability, mental fortitude, and the extent that they have embodied the principles of kendo in manner and movement.

Candidates are divided into groups of four. Each candidate does two *tachiai* (bouts), and must use these opportunities to stand out in the crowd. The performance needs to shine above candidates from the previous and forthcoming groups. To "stand out", mastery of technical skills is a given; but the higher the rank, the more your spirit needs to resonate. If your performance is ordinary and you fail to leave your mark, you will also fail the examination.

## 4. Tidy appearance and proper *reihō*

Judges will pay close attention to your attire, as this is considered to be a reflection of your mind. For example, a *hakama* looks untidy if the back is lower than the front, if the pleats are not crisp, or if the *kendō-gi* is puffed-out at the rear. These things may not have a direct effect on your kendo performance *per se*, but you will look sloppy, and this will influence examiner perception of you. High-ranked practitioners are expected to have an suitable air of grace and dignity, and this is reflected in your posture and manner of dress. Prepare carefully, and make sure you look the part. Scruffy appearance is totally unacceptable.

During the grading, you need to show what level of understanding you have attained, and whether or not this understanding is genuine. Your behaviour and mannerisms should indicate elegance and confidence, but cannot be superficial. The examiners will look closely to see whether your manners and bearing are feigned, or have been cultivated in your training to the degree that they are a natural part of you are. Examiners will not be fooled by

empty acts of propriety.

Those who train regularly will be able to effortlessly perform the series of movements starting from the *taitō* position (*shinai* held at the left hip) through to *sonkyo*. Nothing should be forced, and movements must synchronized with your opponent. Good manners show that you have a serious attitude towards kendo, and this is requisite for high-ranking practitioners. Attire and manners reflect your mental attitude in everyday life, so pay as much attention to honing this in your daily practices as you do for developing your techniques.

## 5. *Sonkyo* is crucial for an effective strike

Some people think that *sonkyo* is simply squatting down and standing up afterwards. The quality of *sonkyo* indicates whether or not you have the ability to control the opponent and produce excellent strikes before the bout even commences.

It has been said that *sonkyo* requires the posture and mindset of a lion. When you do *sonkyo*, your spirit needs to be replete like a lion stalking its prey and getting ready to pounce. Correct *sonkyo* requires a sturdy back and legs. This enables *ki* to be concentrated in the abdomen. Without a strong core, *sonkyo* may become unstable and it will be difficult to remain centred by focusing the *ki* in your gut.

Tense your lower abdomen when squatting down, and keep the tension there until you stand up. Many people relax too much and stand up at the commencement of the bout in an unfocused and flimsy state. They still have a desire to attack their opponent, but body and mind are not in sync. Failing to realise the importance of being primed at the time of *sonkyo* means that your opponent will be a step ahead of you.

When I attended a nationwide seminar, the instructor said, "*Sonkyo* should be just like smoke rising from incense." This means that your neck, back and waist need to be extended and straight, just like incense smoke rising towards the sky. Your movements must be fluid and continuous, like a steady stream of smoke rising from the burning tip of the incense stick, wafting away into the atmosphere.

Be mindful when doing *sonkyo*, especially when training with your sensei. To this end, you cannot go wrong if you adhere to the protocols of the Nippon Kendo Kata. If you follow the lead of the *motodachi* (*uchidachi*), you will have a meaningful *keiko* with perfectly synchronised *ki* (*ai-ki*).

## 6. Elements of *datotsu*

*Kamae*, *seme*, striking opportunity, *waza* selection, strikes, and *zanshin* are executed in a seamless flow, which is then evaluated as a *yūkō-datotsu* (valid strike).

### (1) Kamae

The word *kamae* (fighting stance) means "To have the proper posture and attitude to react to any situation." *Kamae* greatly influences your striking movements, so honing your *kamae* as well as techniques is a must. It is often said that if the "*kamae* is alive" it allows attacking at any time, or facilitates smooth and instantaneous movement. It is the ideal stance that is unimpeded, natural, and explosive.

*Kamae* consists of two parts: *mi-gamae* (body) and *ki-gamae* (mind/spirit). If you stand up straight with feet shoulder width apart and not spread to far, the upper

and lower body will be united and stable. Endeavour to make your *kamae* look big as you stand up from *sonkyo* by relaxing your shoulders, opening your chest, and positioning your ears over your shoulders. The easiest way to open up your chest is to pull your shoulder blades closer together. Position your arms as if you were cradling a baby so that you have enough leeway to manipulate the *shinai* freely.

The position of the left fist is vital in *kamae*. It should be approximately one fist's width away from the body with the joint at the base of the left thumb facing the navel. Some people are tall, some are short, thin, or heavyset. All should have the hands in the correct position regardless of build, but develop a *kamae* that best suits your physique. Your body must be stable, and you should find it easy to lift the *shinai* overhead with the left hand.

Examinees usually look uncomfortable at gradings. Because they are worried about how their *kamae* looks, their upper body becomes tense. Superficial postures can be compared to artificial flowers. They may look pretty at a glance, but if you take a closer look, you realise that they are not real. What is the difference? It's the "fragrance"—artificial flowers don't have any. Strive to develop a *kamae* that shows your intensity of spirit and grace. This is fragrance in the context of *kamae*.

The eyes greatly influence your *kamae*. If you look as if you are staring down from the top of a small hill with a straight back and relaxed shoulders, you will not only be able to manoeuvre freely, you will also be able to pressurise your opponent.

## (2) *Hassei* (Vocalisation)

One of the characteristics of kendo is the constant shouting. There are two kinds of *hassei*: yelling out the target as you strike; and *kakegoe*, which are vocalisations to boost your morale and intimidate your opponent. Vocalisation also increases your concentration, and centres your mind. *Hassei* that emanates from a replete spirit and single-minded resolve is genuine and strong. I believe that it transforms into some kind of invisible power that penetrates the opponent's mind and unsettles them.

It is effective to exhale from your lower abdomen while emitting a deep, resonating yell. Yelling is one of the important techniques of kendo, so pay attention to your *hassei* at training. It is directly related to your posture, and will be substantial if you learn to use the muscles in your lower abdomen while keeping your shoulders relaxed. If your posture is flawed, you will not be able to store energy in the lower abdomen, resulting in a muffled scream which will be ineffectual. Many people think it is acceptable to yell at any time, but there are distinct intervals (*maai*) from where you should and should not shout. It must be done at a safe *maai*, for the simple reason that when you have exhausted your shout you will need to inhale. This will leave you unstable and vulnerable. If you let out an almighty yell from the optimum striking distance, you risk being struck as you breathe in again.

The reason why we shout as we strike the target is to concentrate power into the attack on the point of impact and also to augment momentum for the follow through. This makes the technique decisive.

There are many teachings in kendo that talk of "*a-un no kokyū*". This is referring to the importance of matching your breathing with that of the opponent. It can also mean the stress and intonation of the vocalisation when you attack. For example, if you strike your opponent's *men*, the open-mouthed "*a*" part of the exhalation is right at the start with "*me*". This is seamlessly followed by the closed-mouth "*un*" part of the vocalisation with "*n*" (*me--nnnnn*!) Not only is it important to articulate both sounds, but they should be short, sharp, and the pitch raised at the end.

✷ By doing so, your abdomen will tighten, and your left foot snaps up faster. Your voice should lingers like the ring of a bell resonating after being struck.

## (3) From *tōma* to *shokujin* (blades touching); from *shokujin* to *kojin* (blades crossing) and *issoku-itto-no-ma*

• **Closing the *maai***

There is a maxim, "Feel as if you are close to your opponent, but make them feel far away from you." Of course, physically speaking this is not actually possible, so why is this expression heard so often in kendo? It actually refers to more to mental distance rather than physical distance, and maintaining a sense of psychological superiority over the opponent. You pressurise (*seme*) your opponent and strike the instant an opening arises. To do this, you must be able to gauge the exact distance from where to launch the attack in the physical sense, and be prepared to unleash with total conviction in the psychological sense.

Both start the process of *seme-ai* (pressurising each other) from the distant interval (*tōma*). The *maai* shrinks to *shokujin* (touching), then *kojin* (crossing), and then to the one-step one-sword interval (*issoku-ittō-no-ma*). The tension increases as the *maai* is closed and you enter the *uchima*—the optimal distance from where a strike can

21

be made; not too far, and not too close.

Examinees are often seen standing with their feet planted flat on the floor. Maybe they are too focused on their *kamae* and forget about their feet. Standing flat-footed and shouting "*Yaa, yaa!*" will never intimidate an opponent. Once you rise from the start line, look to close the distance with strong enough *ki* to force your opponent to retreat. This will allow you to enter their territory. It is important that you do not waver in your resolve. As you close in, you may experience distracting thoughts or fear of being struck. This will cloud your mind and make you hesitate, leaving you susceptible to being struck instead. Whatever it takes, you must purge these thoughts from your mind. Be resolute and positive. Exuding a sense of determination and belief in yourself will rile your adversary.

### • *Seme*

From centuries ago, teachings such as "don't strike and win; win and strike", or "the one who wins the battle of *seme* has the right to strike" have been an integral part of budo training. Sensei will advise us to pay more attention before striking, an indication that the process of *seme* is more important than the final attack. Furthermore, an important concept in kendo is to *seme* with *ki* but strike with *ri*. Or, win with *ki*, strike with *ri*. *Ri* is the prescribed theoretical and technical rules of kendo. The act of *seme* is to create an opportunity to strike. Thus, to win or *seme* with *ki* means to actively seek and create holes in the opponent's defences, or lure them into striking through applying psychological and physical pressure. The act of *seme* requires subtle movements of the tip of the sword (*kensen*), as well as the body and feet. When your opponent feels the pressure and becomes agitated, it is a sign that your *seme* is actually having an effect.

In many cases, however, your *seme* may not be effective. You need to evoke a sense of fear and doubt in your opponent's mind, making them think that you are going to strike them at any given moment. This will make them disconcerted. The ability to apply powerful *seme* cannot be mastered overnight.

The judges will not miss subtle changes in the examinees' minds; they will watch carefully to see who is winning the battle of *seme*, and who is dominating the other. They use this information to decide who passes or fails.

A wonderful thing about kendo is that elder sensei can beat younger, faster kendoka. This is possible by not relying on speed, but by incorporating two elements into your kendo: "experience" and "*kiryoku*" (mental power). You will lose your physical prowess as you get older, but your *kiryoku* becomes stronger over the years. Eventually, your *seme* will start showing through the tip of your *shinai* like a magic force flowing from a wand. This concentration of energy will compensate for your declining speed. Strong *seme* only becomes possible when various factors come together. These factors take years to develop and are a reflection of your maturity in kendo.

The following quote from Saimura Gorō-sensei, a Hanshi 10-dan known as a "sword saint" of the twentieth century, demonstrates the importance of *seme*: "No matter how fast your *waza* is, it is created in your mind first. If you can control your own mind, by extension you can control your opponent, and the right *waza* will be born." He is explaining how *waza* is an extension of *seme*. Making a seamless transition from *seme* to *waza* is something all kenshi need to strive for.

• **Controlling the centre**

In order to *seme* effectively, you must first control the centre. One of the main methods to do this is through manipulation of the *shinai*. To score a valid strike, the movement of the *kensen* is crucial. Keeping the *kensen* around the centreline, apply pressure from above, below, and from the left and right sides of the *shinai*. If you can remain psychologically and physically primed, and can pressurise your opponent without veering from the centre, your kendo will not only appear strong, it WILL be strong.

There are several ways to take control of the centre: *hari-waza* (slapping the *shinai*), *osae-waza* (suppressing), *maki-waza* (rolling), and moving the body. There are also variations in *kamae* such as taking a higher or lower stance, or holding the *shinai* with a rigid or soft grip depending on the opponent. It is important to know which *kamae* to use for each situation.

Is everything okay as long as the *kensen* is control of the centreline? Not yet. Your mind should be in the centre as well. Your left hand reflects your mind: if your left hand is shaky, the tip of the *shinai* will naturally move away from the centre. Saimura Gorō-sensei said, "When your left hand moves, you've lost even if you're not struck." Therefore, controlling the centre with the left hand is of the essence. In other words, it is the left hand that guides the *kensen*.

Many practitioners misunderstand the idea of having "power in the *kensen*". Strength in the *kensen* means flexibility. For example, even if your opponent tries to push your *shinai* down from the *omote* (your left) side, you can return the flick back to the centre effortlessly without forcibly pushing back. Also, if your opponent tries to execute a meaningless *waza*, you can thrust the tip of the *shinai* towards their throat (*mukae-tsuki*) and let them know that it was not an opening. This is what being flexible means. Often, people do *mukae-tsuki* to nullify the opponent's strike because they were caught unawares. Kenshi who do not flinch in the face of their opponent's strike deserve credit, but it is not good to do *mukae-tsuki* as an evasive move. It shows that you are unable to take advantage of the openings in your opponent's movements. *Mukae-tsuki* to control an opponent's strike is important, but so is the ability to react flexibly and counter with *debana-waza*, *suriage-waza* or *kaeshi-waza*.

If you only employ *mukae-tsuki* to avoid getting struck, you are essentially saying that you are not flexible enough to do any other *waza*. The expression "If you only do *tsuki*, your *waza* will die", warns people against such an approach. (This is a play on words. "*Tsuki*" from the verb *tsukiru* also means to "exhaust" or "be finished".)

• **Maintaining your own rhythm**
As you close in on your opponent little by little, you will feel a degree of mental tension. Strive to keep your

rhythm while disrupting your opponent's, and make them move according to your dictation.

As you face your opponent and the distance gets incrementally closer, the desire to strike builds. At this stage you are still on an even footing with your opponent. The secret to success in breaking the deadlock is to get into a confident mental state. If you are too desperate to strike, however, you will lose your composure and be distracted by your opponent's movements. That is to say, if you are not composed, you will be unable to determine whether the openings in your opponent's *kamae* and movements are real, or intentionally posed as a trap to lure you in. You could be suckered in to making a careless strike leaving you open to *debana-waza* or *ōji-waza*. This will tell the judges that your opponent is in control of the bout.

Are openings a result of your *seme*, or were they created intentionally to put you in a false sense of security? There is a huge difference between a strike made after creating the opening, and one that happens to connect through random chance. Intention is the key here, but remember that a strong opponent also has their own intentions, and you need to be able to discern what is real, and what is not.

In *Gorin no Sho*, Miyamoto Musashi wrote that

there are two kinds of "seeing": *ken* and *kan*. He said that *ken* is weak and *kan* is strong. *Ken* only sees the surface, but *kan* looks deeper into the opponent's mind. If your opponent intentionally creates an opening, be patient and hold your *kamae*. That way you will be able to keep in your rhythm. After seeing through the trap, the opponent will react if you take a few steps forward. This is essentially disrupting their rhythm. They will then try to regain their composure, and in some cases will carelessly strike you instead. Take advantage of this opportunity and counter with *debana-waza* or *ōji-waza*. This will certainly impress the judges. Conversely, if you try to force your opponent to act but to no avail, this could work against you if you become frustrated. You must be patient. This mental battle is important, and the examiners appreciate it at examinations for the higher *dan* grades. Understand that patience is of the essence.


## (4) Striking opportunities and *waza* selection

### • Initiating attacks

Often I hear people say, "You won't pass a grading if you don't strike *men*", or "You shouldn't strike *dō*". Admittedly, *men* is widely considered the cornerstone of kendo *waza*, but the four valid targets are *men*, *kote*, *dō* and *tsuki*. As such, you should not focus solely on *men*. Be flexible and seize any opportunity that presents itself. As easy as it sounds, everybody struggles with this. I read somewhere, "Listen carefully and you will hear a sound; but even if you clear your mind you will still not be able to hear your opponent's thoughts. It's the same with bells. You can keep hoping for it to ring, but hoping is not enough. You need to actually ring it physically to make the sound. To make your opponent's heart sing, *you need to move it first.*" In other words, be proactive and create your chances.

Many examinees have good *kamae* and energy, but they do not take the initiative. I often see matches where examinees stand up from *sonkyo*, build up their energy, and then try to strike. Conversely, some are so keen to initiate attacks that they strike as soon as they see their opponent move. Sometimes both examinees keep trying to cut each other with the same *waza*. Or, they think they need to strike *men* first and then *kote*. This is all counterproductive.

If you wait until you stand up from *sonkyo* to focus your *ki*, it is already too late. Your spirit must be replete when you are bowing to your opponent. That way, you have already taken the initiative as your rise from *sonkyo*.

In high-level kendo, taking the initiative is the determining factor for victory. Few can remain completely calm when an opponent manoeuvres confidently into their space. Most people feel compelled to react. This is why *seme* is at the crux of kendo. By initiating attacks, more opportunities are created. You need to train hard to fully understand this.

When attacking or defending, or when you become confused and freeze, the state of your mind is clearly evident in your actions. Look for these psychological and physical clues in your opponent, and then select the correct *waza* to capitalise on the hole in their defence. Good opportunities will arise only when you initiate them. Waiting will achieve nothing; create chances yourself.

## • *Waza* born of *seme*

*Waza* can be categorised into two groups: *shikake-waza* (off-the-mark techniques) and *ōji-waza* (counter techniques). *Shikake-waza* requires you to strike the instant your opponent reacts, or is thinking about reacting, to your advances. *Ōji-waza* is the execution of *waza* in response to the opponent's attack. Still, successful *ōji-waza* is only possible by applying pressure and making them attack. Good *ōji-waza* is not reactionary, but purposeful. Whilst applying pressure, give your opponent the impression that they have room to attack. Invite them in, and strike when they are committed.

Why is it that people end up striking when they are under pressure? It is because the situation is not in their favour, and they feel an urgency to turn things around and regain control. To their detriment, they come to the hasty conclusion that striking is the only way out of the hole. As a result, attacks are initiated without proper mental preparation, and the hole gets deeper.

## (5) Strikes

Landing a valid technique during a grading has considerable bearing on the result. You are required strike the targets accurately, but it must be a logical conclusion to the preceding process of *seme*. Strikes should conform to the prescribed basics, be full of energy and spirit, and the movements before and after need to "touch the judges' hearts". You will not move anybody unless you throw everything into the strike.

What decides whether strikes are considered valid or not is a monumental concern. Let us take *men* as an example. The instant your *shinai* makes contact with the opponent's *men*, this is a hit but the strike is not yet valid. It is only considered valid when the entire process is completed. To complete the strike means continuing the momentum after making contact, and following through while maintaining your physical and mental posture. The point of impact itself is obviously important, but completing the striking process is the deciding factor in its validity.

Taking *ippon* is an absolute necessity in a grading, but will not count if it is accidental. The most effective way to prepare in *keiko* is to know the importance of scoring the *shodachi* (first strike) in all of your bouts. Be determined to take first blood no matter who you face, and be sure to complete the strike.

Another vital aspect is to build up *tame* (tension) before you strike. Often you will hear sensei comment, "Your strikes don't have *tame*". What is *tame*? It is difficult to explain, but I interpret it as being primed and stalking your opponent. The moment s/he is startled and begins to move, mercilessly seize the start of their movement by unleashing all of that built up pressure. If you are too eager to strike, you are likely to execute *waza* before your opponent moves. If you wait too long, you will freeze and will not be able to take advantage of good opportunities. *Tame* can be understood as lying between excessive eagerness and being settled. The only way to be able to strike with *tame* is through constant *keiko*.

At a grading, strikes that are not strong or sharp enough are unlikely to be regarded highly. People tend to think that good strikes are determined by control of the hands. While subtle manipulation of the hands (*tenouchi*) is indeed instrumental in making the strike crisp and decisive, use of the feet should not be forgotten. The right foot is the "*seme* foot", and the left is the "power foot". When you strike, kick off with the left foot and stamp forward with the right as you snap the left foot up immediately at the point of impact. The harder you

push off with your left foot, the more resounding the right foot stamp will be.

## 7. Your greatest weapon is your spirit

Overwhelm your opponent with your energy and spirit, and then execute *waza*. You only have a very short time in examinations to show your stuff. To successfully demonstrate a strong, indomitable spirit, it is useful to imagine that the bout is a real duel with live blades; i.e. if you lose, you lose your life. Strikes must be made with *sutemi* (absolute conviction). The spirit that burns hottest will decide the outcome.

Unsuccessful candidates will feel dejected. "Even though I hit my opponent, I still didn't pass. Where did I go wrong?" Again, allow me to summarise the criteria for scoring a valid point: replete spirit, correct posture, *zanshin*. An indomitable spirit is the foundation of your *waza*. If this is missing, you may hit the target but it will never be considered a valid cut.

The following incidents demonstrate what I mean by "spirit". At the Chiba Prefecture Enbu Championship in April, 2008, I thought that my *men* and *kote* strikes were good enough to score. My sensei who observed the match said so, too. Hanshi 8-dan Iwadate Saburo-sensei, however, said that

I lacked "proper energy". I did not understand what he meant, but had chances to receive instruction from him several times afterwards. Each time, he told me that I "still lacked energy". Right before my 8-dan grading, Iwadate-sensei told me to put my fighting spirit on show. Following his advice, I was able to pass 8-dan at that grading.

Another time, I participated in a grading seminar in Tokyo. The point was driven home how important it is to face your opponent with an "unrelenting spirit". I was told that if the level of the opponent's energy is 100, mine should be 120. If the opponent's energy is 120, then mine should be 150. The lesson here is that one's energy should always exceed that of one's opponent.

Kendo techniques originated in sword fights to the death. Everybody would surely fight with all of their might in mortal combat. Promotion examinations are no different. Once you stand up, you must show greater spirit than the other candidates. Your spirit must be felt by your opponent and the judges at the same time.

Those with a strong spirit show it in their eyes—they are full of life. On the contrary, those with a dull spirit have eyes that look weak. Overwhelm the opponent with your spirit, and when holes manifest in their mind, *kamae* or actions, strike with absolute conviction. Even if the strike is not valid, it will still have value.

Those who suffocate their opponent with spirit and strike with ruthless conviction stand out. Remember that the follow through after the strike is also crucial. The whole process of assailing, striking, and following through for the next stanza is enacted in one seamless movement. To this end, an indomitable spirit is the lifeblood of kendo.

## 8. Patience after the strike

Judges pay attention to how a match proceeds after a valid strike has been scored. If you are able to execute a successful strike first, that will give you a mental advantage; but, you may start to panic if one is scored against you first! Thus, it really is important to take the first strike. One of the criteria that examiners are required to consider is the ratio of valid points. Let us assume that you score a palpable valid point, the way you continue the fight after this will determine whether you pass or fail. You may feel a strong urge to get another, but if you hastily try to strike while the iron is hot and end up getting hit instead, your former *ippon* will be considered moot.

A secret teaching of the Yagyū-ryū school of swordsmanship tells that, "Following the lead of your opponent is the key to victory." It sounds counter-intuitive, but I interpret this as meaning that you must try and make your opponent strike at you. You are "following their lead" because you are "leading them to lead..." In other words, you must call the shots. In this sense, patience is vital after completing a successful strike. Allow them to show how desperate they are.

Do not dilute your decisive technique with meaningless, superfluous strikes afterwards. If the match ends as it is, your opponent will lose because of your *ippon*. Knowing this, s/he will become agitated, and impatient to get a point back. Hold on and suppress their attempts. If you can respond to your opponent exactly in the way described in Miyamoto Musashi's teaching "*makura no osae*" (nipping the enemy's technique in the bud), it will make him or her even more frantic. Desperation leads to instability, and even openings to pick off at will. This presents a good opportunity to execute various *waza*. If you can do this, you will rise above the rest of the examinees. Consequently, patience is the critical difference between those who pass, and those who do not.

## 9. Keeping it together at the venue

Maintain your concentration until the end of the exam is a big factor in the result. All candidates have subjected themselves to a rigorous training regime to prepare, even though family and work commitments limit time in the dojo. Taking exams is also a financial burden because of transportation costs and fees, etc. Every time you fail you need to pay more, which is all the more reason for wanting to pass.

You arrive at the venue determined to make it work. So far, so good. The problem is that you are likely to meet acquaintances once you are there. You enjoy the reunion and a nice chat. Even though you have been training hard and trying to maintain your focus, you get distracted and risk failure because of it. You might think it rude but refrain from talking to others. Never compromise your focus.

After passing the first stage of the 8-dan examination, I sat in a seat in the upper tier of the venue, and refused to talk to anybody before the second stage. To be honest, I felt could not help but feel nervous. Everybody does, but you must somehow learn to ignore your anxiety. If you can overcome your nervousness, passing the exam becomes more realistic.

## 10. *Keiko* after the grading

Everybody trains hard for exams, and funnily enough, those who pass suddenly become even more enthusiastic about training. Contrarily, those who fail may lose motivation. Some may even take a break from training for a while. We all know how disappointing it is to have your dreams shattered, but the important thing is to continue training. If you stop *keiko* because you failed, it will appear as though the whole purpose of your study of kendo is for accumulating rank. Such a reaction is lamentable. As much as it hurts, turn the pain into motivation, and start preparing yourself for the next test. Should you fail and experience disappointment, get back on your horse and train even harder. This is what kendo is supposed to be about.

Another thing I would like to point out is that you should never complain about the result. Comments along the lines of "My opponent did weird kendo" is just an excuse. They are probably saying exactly the same thing to their friends about you. Blaming your opponents for your failures means that you are blissfully unaware of your own lack of ability.

Those who pass, on the other hand, sometimes say, "I was lucky that I had a good opponent." This is the same as claiming that you were successful only because your opponent was accommodating, and it was just sheer good fortune. You might as well be admitting that you do not deserve the grade. Kendo requires working with others, but placing the onus of success or failure on your opponent is not acceptable. It is a cop out. Train hard enough so that it doesn't matter who you come up against.

# CHAPTER 2
# *Cultivating your own kendo philosophy*

We "play" sports, but training in the traditional Japanese budo arts is known as "*keiko*". The literal meaning of "*keiko*" is to "ponder the ancient ways" or "study ancient things". In other words, it means to contemplate the teachings of our predecessors, and emphasises the importance of one's mental attitude towards the arts. As practitioners of kendo, we need to be cognisant of our responsibility to preserve the traditions of this valuable culture, and pass it on to future generations. By reconsidering the meaning of *keiko*, and training ourselves accordingly, I believe that we will be able to develop an even more vibrant and relevant kendo philosophy for the people of the times.

## 1. *Kirikaeshi* and *uchikomi* foster strength

*Kirikaeshi* and *uchikomi* are important types of *keiko* that help to solidify the foundations of your kendo. It is hard for regular people to secure enough time to train due to work or family commitments, so most end up doing mainly *ji-geiko* (*gokaku-geiko*), and not so much *kirikaeshi*. You must make an effort to do *kirikaeshi* and *uchikomi*.

Ideal *kirikaeshi* is described as being "big, strong, quick, and light". When a beginner does *kirikaeshi*, it needs to be executed in a big, correct motion, and becomes gradually stronger with time. The more you train, the quicker, lighter and more graceful the movement will become.

*Kirikaeshi* is a combination of *shōmen* (front) and *sayū* (diagonal) *men* strikes, and is a method of *keiko* that helps you master the most basic movements. I often see kendo practitioners strike *men*, then take four steps forward striking left and right *men*, five back, and then finish a final *men* strike. This is the basic method of *kirikaeshi* for instructing beginners. Originally, it was never decided how many strikes would be made; instead the attacker would follow the *motodachi*'s lead, strike however many times was necessary, and then finish when they were allowed to.

*Uchikomi-geiko* is where the *motodachi* intentionally creates openings to strike in succession. It is crucial that each and every strike meets the requirements for a valid strike. The attacker has to constantly keep posture, spirit, *maai*, sharpness of *tenouchi* (hand manipulation in the grip), footwork, and breath control in mind, and make each strike count. It is easy to say that each strike should be a *yūkō-datotsu*, but in actuality this is very difficult to achieve.

When I was a *tokuren* (riot squad) member in the police, I visited various places for *keiko*, and received valuable instruction from many different sensei. Back then, *keiko* ended with *uchikomi* or *kakari-geiko*, and *kirikaeshi*. We would say "Thank you very much" when struck by the sensei, and then launch into *uchikomi* and *kirikaeshi*. If the content and quality of our *keiko* was poor, *uchikomi* and *kirikaeshi* would last forever. We would be left completely out of breath and gasping for air with absolutely no energy left. This is the kind of *keiko* that helps you nurture real strength. At the time I thought it was unbearable, but now I am truly grateful for the strict instruction.

These days, not many people ask for *uchikomi* and *kirikaeshi* after *keiko*, which is a shame. I wonder how many people understand the importance of *uchikomi* and *kirikaeshi*. Doing *ji-geiko* alone will not help you develop strength. *Uchikomi* and *kirikaeshi* are hard, but that is the very reason why it has benefits afterwards. I imagine most people want to avoid it, but *uchikomi* and *kirikaeshi* will lead to significant improvement even if your practice time is limited.

Basic training is the quickest way to improve. There is a teaching that goes, "By learning the basics, you will create a foundation to apply the basics to. To reach a higher-level of application, you need to learn the basics even more thoroughly." So, if you are at a loss as to what to do, go back to basics. In fact, go back to basics even if you are not at a loss.

## 2. "Two-faced" *keiko*

The only way to pass a grading examination is to train. To do this efficiently, plan how much time to spend on what, and systematically build your basic strength. Sometimes you will not pass an exam even though you have what it takes technically. Sometimes, you just can't demonstrate your true ability. One of the possible reasons could be that the content of your training is removed from what the actual examination is like.

Specifically, you should refrain from doing "two-faced" *keiko*. In other words, always give your best regardless of the situation. Everybody tries hard during *keiko* with their sensei. Unfortunately this is not consistent, and people have a tendency to take it easy when practising with people who are either of the same grade or lower than themselves. They forget their sensei's advice and continue repeating their flawed routine when not being watched. In Japanese, this is known as "*hoi hoi kendō*" (mindless kendo); it lacks seriousness. Kenshi who train like this will not succeed. Even if they are fortunate enough to pass, I doubt that their grade represents their true ability. They are guaranteed to experience extreme hardship at future gradings.

No matter who you are training with, or what their grade is, follow the guidance you receive from your sensei. This is what makes your kendo better. It may be difficult to break your sensei's composure with your *seme*, but if you face those of a similar or lower grade with the same kind of passion and determination, you will land strikes that everybody, including the victim, will be in awe of.

There is no *keiko* better than that done with *aiki*, where both practitioners are fully committed and giving 100%. It is always meaningful no matter how short the *keiko* is. *Keiko* that lacks seriousness is a complete waste of time, and will not be thought highly of. There is no *keiko* uglier than when the two protagonists are bereft of *ki*.

The judges do not have time to watch you for five minutes, let alone ten, so in your daily *keiko*, you need to focus on scoring valid strikes in a short amount of time. In the exam, you will not have the leeway you normally have in *keiko*. So, make your examination objectives the basis for your *keiko*.

## 3. The right attitude

### (1) *Keiko* with kenshi of a higher level

When doing *keiko* with high-level sensei, you should feel grateful for the instruction. At the same time, you need to feel "equal" when it comes to scoring the *shodachi*, and single-mindedly aim for taking first blood. In other words, think of *keiko* as *ippon-shōbu*—a one-point match. Even if you take the *shodachi* against the sensei, never let your guard down, or feel validated because you got the first point. Never back down, block, or avoid cuts. Give 100%, and attack whenever you can.

This means avoid doing deceitful or cunning kendo like you might do in a competition. Instead, face your sensei head on and do the best kendo that you can. If you are too focused on simply finding gaps to strike and avoid getting hit, this indicates that your mind is preoccupied with the result. *Keiko* like this is meaningless and cheap.

Moreover, doing *keiko* as if you are the same level is out of the question. Trainings these days are different from that of my youth. It is often impossible to tell the difference between the sensei and the student. The student merely waits for the sensei to attack, and then tries to half-heartedly pick off their *kote*. Come what may, attack with total commitment; after *keiko* you should be drained and have nothing left. This kind of *keiko* leads to improvement. Even if it is short, it is rich in content. *Keiko* with your sensei should leave you completely out of breath.

## (2) *Keiko* with kenshi of the same level

*Keiko* with people of the same level (*gokaku-geiko*) is just as important as *keiko* with sensei. People of a similar age and level are matched against each other in gradings, so *keiko* with them helps you to determine your capabilities. Think of *gokaku-geiko* as a mock exam. Pay attention to your posture, *seme*, strikes, and *zanshin*. It is a perfect opportunity to test your patience, whether or not your *waza* is effective, and so on. If you feel content with the overall *keiko*, it means that you are one step closer to the *dan* you want to achieve.

When doing *gokaku-geiko*, it is counterproductive to want to strike and avoid being struck through blocking, dodging and ducking. If you get hit, it means your opponent has found a weakness, and you should take a lot away from that. Do *keiko* with humility and gratitude.

### (3) *Keiko* with kenshi of a lower level

There are two methods of *keiko* with kenshi of a lower level: one where you try to improve your skills; the other where you try to improve your opponent's skills.

First, how can you use this type of *keiko* to your advantage and improve your own skills? The answer is simple: don't take it easy. You still need *aiki* and to be equally committed. Some people never do their best when facing lower level opponents. This is meaningless *keiko* which only satisfies people's hunger for seemingly scoring with ease.

Engaging in *keiko* with lower-level kenshi is important for learning *riai*—the principles behind the techniques. It is also a perfect opportunity to experiment with *seme* as well as improve your striking skills. Undertake *keiko* with the understanding that it is the best chance to learn striking opportunities. In other words, reassure yourself that you need this to learn how to put theory into practice.

The second type of *keiko* augments improvement in the lower level practitioner. Known as "*hikitate-geiko*", it teaches *kakarite* the joy of making a successful strike, as well as the right timing for attacking. The *kakarite* usually trains with a certain goal in mind, such as trying to get a handle on basic techniques. This means that *motodachi* plays an important role in guiding them in the right direction. During *hikitate-geiko*, *motodachi* makes *kakarite* feel the severity of *seme*, and what constitutes a solid strike. This experience will help them improve tremendously later on.

Both you and your opponent are like a whetstone, using each other to polish technique and mind. When you are *motodachi*, it goes without saying that you have a responsibility to help *kakarite* improve both technically and mentally. When you are leading *shidō-geiko*, make *kakarite* think, "I'm glad I asked him/her to train with me. I want to ask again." The last thing you want is to have them think, "I never want to train with that sensei again." Prepare properly and take care not to run an uninspiring training session. Keep it energetic and meaningful for all concerned.

Use the opportunity to polish your "sense of intuition", or "*kizashi*". Openings identified with *kizashi* are not visible, but are felt in the mind from the slight fluctuations in *ki*. The most fulfilling interaction in kendo is having the confidence to attack based on *kizashi*. This only comes from being able to probe deeply into your opponent's mind. If you strike aimlessly, you will never be able to improve your sensitivity to the ebbs and flow of *ki*.

## 4. Forging *ki*

Every kendo practitioner has a "wall of *ki*", but that wall is thin and fragile without enough training. The more training you do, and the more experience you gain, the thicker and stronger the wall becomes. When doing *keiko* with a kenshi with a high *dan* grade, you will often find yourself unable to strike no matter how hard you try. Their invisible wall closes in on you, suffocates you, and leaves you unable to move. Then you end up getting struck instead.

It is easy to understand the strikes that judges prefer—they are the ones where the *ki* of the striker is strong. Striking opportunities that arise through the build up of *ki* are regarded highly; whereas strikes executed with speed but without intent or feeling are considered merely as "hitting" and are not given much credence.

An effective way to nurture your wall of *ki* is to unleash it against a more experienced practitioner. *Ki* will bounce back at you. This will allow your *ki* to grow slowly but surely, and your wall will get thicker and stronger over time.

When attacking a high level sensei, even if you feel pressured by their *ki*, and you know that you are bound to get struck and countered, you must never back away. This is the only way to forge your *ki*.

Sensei will tell you to train with people much stronger than you, and to attack them without hesitation. This is because they know that *ki* can only be cultivated through hard work. *Gokaku-geiko* and *keiko* with kenshi less skilled may help you improve your technique, but has little effect in nurturing your *ki*. For this purpose, seeking and challenging stronger kenshi is the only way to go, even though you might be taken apart. Overcome this fear and revel in the hardship.

# 5. Consider "*kyojitsu*"

*Kyo* (emptiness, unprepared) indicates a weakness or an opening. *Jitsu* (being replete with *ki*, prepared) is strength. Never strike at the opponent when s/he is in a state of *jitsu*. Hold on and try to create a hole in their *jitsu* forcefield. The hole, however fleeting, is *kyo*. There are three kinds of openings: in the mind, posture, and movement. These openings are not separate entities, but are closely related. How the hole is created in the clash of wills is a central element in the perceived quality of the strike.

While it is indeed important to identify an opening in your opponent's defences, the process leading to this is paramount. No kenshi willingly shows *kyo*. To elaborate, *jitsu* (one's strength) is worn like armour on the outside, but *kyo* (weakness) is hidden underneath. To find a hidden opening, you need to break through the wall of your opponent's *jitsu*. Your determination to break through is called *sen* (taking the initiative), and *seme* (applying pressure). A beginner's wall of *jitsu* is thin and easily ruptures, but when it comes to trained experts, *jitsu* is stronger and harder to penetrate.

No matter how many times you get repelled by your opponent's forcefield, perseverance and self-belief is required. Even breaking through by one millimetre is a significant feat. Continually training with such determination will give you a foundation to build on into the future. It becomes the driving force behind your *seme*. Once you understand this, you will figure out what kind of *keiko* you need to do.

H9-dan Narazaki Masahiko-sensei said, "It is imperative to find an opening based on *kyojitsu*, but sometimes you need to have enough spirit to face your opponent's *jitsu* with your own *jitsu*, and strike to win." Whether engaging in *keiko* with those who are of the same, higher, or lower level than you, keeping the notion of *kyojitsu* in mind will take you to a different level. It may not bear fruit immediately, but you will reap the rewards later.

When I observe the *keiko* of junior high and high school students these days, they show no inkling that they are supposed to be challenging their opponent. They seem more interested in hanging about to scavenge a lucky strike, rather than working out how to break through the opponent's wall and get them to drop their guard. This is passive, opportunistic kendo. They start by defending themselves, and continue the rest of the match that way. This has a lot to do with the way they are being taught. It is critical, in this sense, for everybody to reconsider the true nature of kendo. Always① probe, always be primed②, and always take③ the initiative.

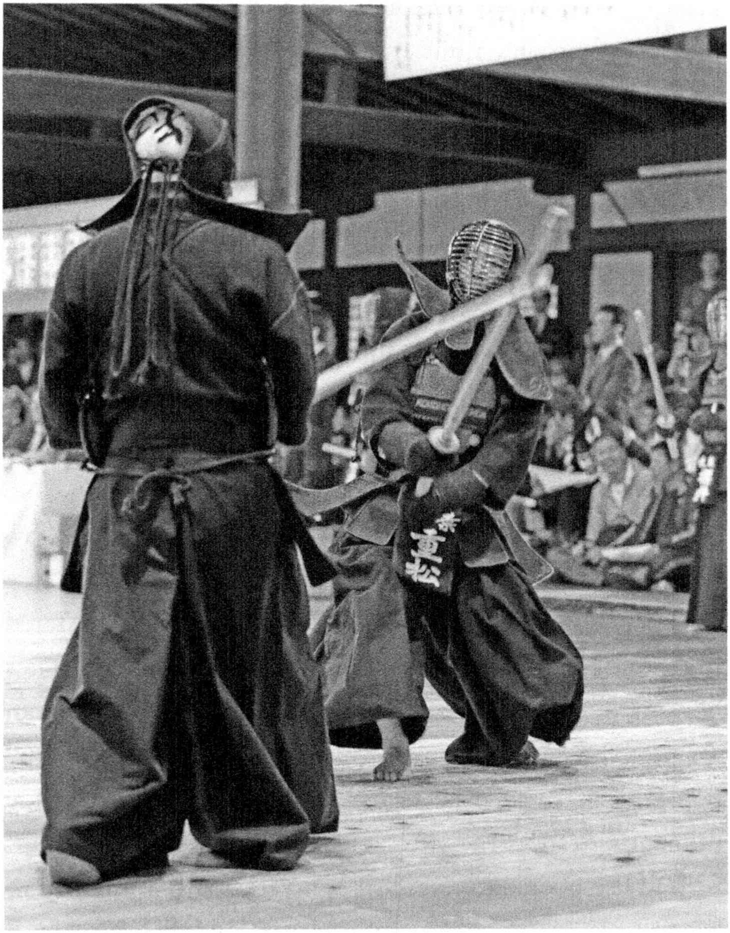
重松

# 6. Does your kendo match your *dan*?

Feeling the pressure to express themselves during gradings, candidates become quite frantic. Judges will evaluate your kendo in accordance with the criteria stated in Article 14 of the "Regulations for Dan/Kyu and Shogo Title Certificates" (All Japan Kendo Federation). It is hard enough to pass a grading, but it is even more difficult to keep doing kendo that matches the grade you receive. Who is judging your grade and ability in the dojo? Nobody announces that s/he holds a certain *dan*. Your true ability is constantly being assessed by your opponents in *keiko*, those waiting to train with you, and those who are just watching. Throw yourself into *keiko* in a way that makes them say, "Of course s/he is X-dan." No matter what happens, your *keiko* must not make them say, "Blimey, does s/he really hold X-dan?"

The criteria for conferring *dan* and *kyū* grades are stated in Article 14 mentioned above. In addition, Article 16 states how many years of training are required before you can attempt the next grade. Why are there such requirements? It means that you need to use the years wisely, and study diligently to meet the criteria for the next level.

I advise people to establish concrete goals, and strive to keep improving to ensure that they can hold their head high after passing. For example, if the grade in question is 5-dan, you should aim for 5.1-dan, 5.2-dan, 5.3-dan, etc. With time and accumulated training you should reach 5.9-dan. This will set you apart from your peers, and will mean your right to that grade is incontrovertible.

## 7. Acknowledging insufficient strikes

Promotion examination or not, everybody can identify what a perfect cut is—assailing your opponent, creating an opening, then striking immediately to take the *ippon*. This is, however, easier said than done simply because the opponent is trying to do the same. You might complain, "I struck my opponent, but they didn't acknowledge it." Such remarks are frequently directed at referees in a lost match, or examiners in a failed exam. The plaintiff sounds as if they are insisting on the validity of a strike because, somehow, they know better.

Everybody strikes their opponent expecting (or hoping) it will be counted as *ippon*. This is subjective, not objective thinking. An ideal *ippon* is one that convinces the opponent as well as referees or examiners. Furthermore, spectators should also be convinced. Doing *keiko* with cuts that are only 99% is never going to be good enough. Always strive for 100% in your regular *keiko*, otherwise you too will end up passing the blame when your attempts are not acknowledged.

## 8. Seek and learn

There are various ways to commit to *keiko* depending on the person, position, and environment. Regardless of your circumstances, try to have clear goals and be passionate about what you do. Many people have to balance training with work and family. In spite of the sacrifices needed, you have to be proactive. If you train with the same people at the same place all of the time, you will become accustomed to that environment, and will lose the sense of tension that should always be present. It will become *keiko* for *keiko*'s sake.

You never know what style your opponent will come at you with in exams or matches. This is why you should leave your comfort zone and go and seek new adversaries. If you can, visit a new place to train at in addition to your usual venue. This will help you learn how to deal with kenshi with different styles, and your kendo will become more versatile. You will also be able to work on unexpected problems that you encounter along the way.

Another matter for consideration is your aspirations for improvement. All kenshi must have a will to learn. There are always seminars and training camps where you can gain useful knowledge. Practise what you learn, and see if it works for you. If it does, consider how you are going to "make it your own". This kind of experimentation will improve your kendo and keep you stimulated.

Unfortunately, there are some high ranked kenshi who are lacking in this learning attitude. Although called "sensei" by those around them, students learning under them have no real role model to follow. As a sensei, this constitutes gross negligence.

Kendo training is a tough path with no end. Even though you may not see light at the end of the tunnel, actively seeking the light anyway is the essence of kendo training. When you become good enough to be referred to as "sensei", you might find yourself wallowing in complacency. Be careful.

## 9. Solitary *keiko*

Through the medium of the *shinai*, you and your opponent teach each other about mutual flaws, which leads to mutual improvement. *Hitori-geiko* (solitary *keiko*) is useful for working on your shortcomings. There are two kinds of *hitori-geiko*: solo training for technical skills, and for developing mental strength.

One of the common exercises is *suburi*. Practice swings are effective for perfecting *tenouchi* and the weight of your strikes. *Suburi* is not just indispensable for beginners, but for anyone who practises kendo. Many kenshi also learn some form of *koryū* (classical martial arts) alongside their regular kendo. This exposes technical and mental aspects of swordsmanship not so evident in the modern martial sport.

Something that can help mental strength is Zen meditation. Swordsmen of old enriched their mental strength through Zen, and disciplined themselves so that they could forge an "immoveable mind". Nurturing dignity and grace necessitates solitary training to keep your mind still. Being surprised and succumbing to fear comes from a movement of the mind, and this is directly connected to your breathing. If you become breathless in the fray, it means that your mind is disturbed.

Breathing techniques are important to master, and currently the most popular style is the *tanden* (lower abdomen) breathing method. Inhale quickly and exhale slowly for as long as possible using your abdominal muscles. You can strengthen your *tanden* this way, and also boost your reserves of *ki*. By enhancing the *ki* in your *tanden*, you will not lose your breath so easily amid the heated exchanges of techniques. You will brim with energy, and it will allow you to attack your opponent without hesitation. For this reason, some people even describe kendo's assailing process as an attempt to disturb each other's breathing.

When inhaling, you are in the state of *kyo*, and vulnerable. It is especially dangerous after you release *kiai*. Inhale quickly so that your opponent does not notice. When tanden > L fist > shinai > kensen

exhaling, this is *jitsu*, and you will be stable and ready to go. Assail your opponent while exhaling. The *ki* you generate in your *tanden* will transfer to your left fist, then to your *shinai*, and will eventually manifest in the tip of your sword. Exhale sharply as you strike. This kind of breathing is critical in kendo. There is a saying that "breathing and *ki* are united". Strengthening your mind and forging *ki* is inextricably linked to the mastery of breathing.

I also recommend remedial physical training. Young kenshi are more dependent on physical strength in *keiko*. You will certainly notice a physical decline as you get older. Many kenshi find that the strikes they used to make from a certain interval (*maai*) gradually become impossible to pull off. You have to make physical adjustments as you get older, and this is where the importance of *ki* becomes more obvious.

*Ki* cannot be developed unless you are training yourself physically, as with the maxim: "A sound mind in a sound body." By training your legs and hips, your *ki* will become more complete, and your *keiko* style will be all the more robust. It is ideal to work out the lower body for endurance, and to continue working on the basics. To this end, the benefits of *hitori-geiko* are immense.

# 10. Discipline your mind in everyday life

Kendo is not confined to the dojo. Of course, the dojo is your main training venue, but it is possible to discipline your mind in your daily life by embracing adversity rather than running away from it. For example, going to *keiko* in the summer even though you know it will be very hot, or standing barefooted on the floor in the winter even though it is extremely cold is hard, and it is only to easy to find an excuse not to. Getting up in the morning is a good way to train your mind to "get hard". I am sure most people rely on an alarm clock to wake up. Why not try jumping out of bed immediately instead of using the snooze function when the alarm goes off? This is like *sutemi*. When you think like this and spring into action at the start of the day, it will have a positive effect on your *keiko*.

"*Zengo saidan*" is a teaching that means, "Yesterday does not matter, neither does tomorrow. What matters is now, so live the moment." Cherishing every second, and every moment helps to develop your *ki*. It is all dependent on your level of motivation for whatever it is that you are doing. If you are trying to foster your spirit, yet decide to skip something that day because you can't be bothered, you will end up becoming a person lacking real grit. In everything, the three *shin* (minds) are important: *hosshin* is motivation;

*kesshin* is determination; *sōzokushin* is continuation.

H9-dan Ogawa Chūtarō-sensei said, "Undertake whatever task you've been given seriously. If you can do that, your kendo ability will never wilt." Even if you have no time to go to the dojo, devise ways of training yourself in the course of your daily life. Rest assured, this will improve your kendo.

## 11. The teaching of *shu-ha-ri*

"*Shu-ha-ri*" is a Japanese teaching frequently mentioned in the world of budo and the tea ceremony. It is said to have been based on a *tanka* (31-syllable Japanese poem) written by Sen no Rikyū—the legendary tea master—for the benefit of a carpenter friend. The *tanka* reads:

> *When using one's tools or obeying formalities in associating with others, forget not the basics. Then, having mastered the fundamentals, break away. Finally, create protocols uniquely your own. But still, never forget the basics.*

In the context of kendo, this expression is used to encourage practitioners to first learn and copy the movements of their sensei, in whom they must have complete faith. Then they must work hard to add their own twist to what they have learned. Finally, they will develop their own philosophy and style. In other words, this expression refers to the order of the training process in kendo.

The following is the definition of each word:

- ***Shu*** — To determine. To not disobey: This means you should observe the teachings of your sensei to the letter. This is the most basic level for learning.
- ***Ha*** — To break with tradition: After fully mastering your sensei's style, you will embark on a journey to test your knowledge and learn new phases and methods not encountered in the *shu* phase. This is the stage of applied techniques.
- ***Ri*** — The completion of *shu*: The final phase of *ri* means to develop your own philosophy based on the sum of what you have learned. In other words, it means transcendence.

Kendoka hone their own style of kendo as their *dan* becomes higher. I still aspire to a style of kendo which emphasises the *shu* stage, irrespective of my rank. Cherishing the basics will make your students and other practitioners want to emulate you. It is to be a role model for *keiko*.

There is another teaching that is similar to s*hu-ha-ri*:

> *You learn applied techniques through acquiring the basics. To reach a higher technical level requires a deeper investigation of the basics.*

We tend to forget the importance of the basics as our kendo advances. Sadly, we cannot learn from our sensei indefinitely, and as one travels further down the path of kendo, fewer people are inclined to point out problems and faults. It is a mistake to stray from orthodox kendo for the sake of pursuing one's own "unique" style. On observing a high-ranking sensei's *keiko*, it may seem as though he or she has moved into the realms of *ha* or *ri*. The truth is that the sensei has simply mastered the basics to such a sublime level, it is unrecognisable to us.

## 12. Instructor qualities

Kendo is a sublimated form of *kenjutsu*, which was created through trial and error by our predecessors. It is a traditional form of Japanese culture that has a long history, and has been passed down through many generations. Instructors are responsible for inheriting the teachings, and correctly conveying the knowledge to future generations. They need to teach "proper kendo", but what does that actually mean? In short, it is the acquisition of technical mastery and cultivation of the mind.

The techniques have to be based on principles underlying the usage of real swords. This necessitates paying attention to *hasuji* (blade angle) and *shinogi* (side of the blade) during *keiko*. Cultivation of the mind is to develop a sense of uprightness, humility, and good manners. "Uprightness" is to act morally; "humility" is to maintain integrity and have a sense of shame; "manners" refers to knowing how to behave appropriately around others.

People seem to have lost sight of these important kendo objectives. They appear to be rather skill-oriented and overly concerned about winning and losing. Why is this so? Perhaps it is because instructors feel that unless their students achieve good results, their value as a teacher will diminish.

Teachings such as "*sossen suihan*" (to set an example worth following) and "*shitei dōgyō*" (students and teachers are on the same path) suggest that a good instructor should take the initiative in *keiko*, and understand what correct, dignified kendo is. They must cultivate their own mind and be able to teach kendo culture without focusing only on techniques.

## 13. Is your instruction appreciated?

When instructing your, you need to make sure that you do not give students reason to say or think things like, "He talks the talk, but he ain't walking the walk."

There is a truism that says, "Vows made in storms are forgotten in the calm." I sometimes see people who, feeling bitter at having failed many examination attempts, instantly become more critical of others the moment they do pass. I almost feel like pointing out that if they know so much, they should have passed much sooner!

As your grade becomes higher you will have more opportunities to teach others. It behoves you to make your kendo something that everybody admires. They will seek your instruction out and model their own kendo on yours. To instruct others is to convey your kendo philosophy, and is a great privilege that you have to be worthy of.

I took my first 8-dan grading in Tokyo in November 2006 when I was 47. I was full of confidence but the result was far from satisfactory. I travelled between Kyoto and Tokyo for the examination, and finally, in Kyoto on May 1, 2009, I passed on my sixth attempt at the age of 50.

After passing the 8-dan examination, I pledged to carry out the following three things:

First, I will keep trying to make my kendo stronger. This means not just having the ability to strike my opponent with technical dexterity. It is to assail opponents with strong *ki*, agitate them so that openings arise, and then seizing that opportunity. This is the kind of kendo I keep working at. I do not attempt a strike unless I can overwhelm my opponent with my *seme* first. To do this, I need to keep building my *ki*. The best way to enhance *ki*

is incessant attacking in *kakari-geiko*. Once you become 8-dan, however, there are fewer opportunities to do this as you are required to be *motodachi*. Therefore, I make it a rule to ask higher-level sensei to train with me three times a month.

Second, I pledged to work on my physical condition so that I can continue to endure rigorous *keiko*. As I use trains, cars, and buses, I feel that my legs are getting weaker, and my basic physical strength is declining as I age. The less physical strength I have, the harder it will be to do kendo, which puts me at risk of injury. After becoming 8-dan, there are many times when you have to be *motodachi* for an extended period of time. It is impossible to perform satisfactory *keiko* without adequate physical strength. As a sturdy body is fundamental to doing kendo, I am working on maintaining core power, and strengthen the legs, back, and abdomen to avoid injury.

Third, I pledged to constantly reflect on my kendo. I failed the 8-dan grading five times. The fact that I failed means that my kendo did not meet the requirements of Article 14 of the "Regulations for Dan/Kyu and Shogo Title Certificates". Fortunately, I was able to receive instruction and advice from many sensei, which helped me pass on my sixth try. Right now I am trying to reflect on my past kendo failures and figure out what caused them. Everybody has flaws. The point of training is to identify and remedy them in an ongoing process. Always seek your own shortcomings and try to fix them.

## 14. Kendo is about developing willpower

Ultimately, kendo depends on willpower. Your skills may improve as time passes, but your body will get weaker. Therefore, if you are too dependent on skills that rely on physical ability, you will eventually reach an impasse. To continue kendo for a long time, you need to master the basics.

Kendo has an image of being "tough" and "hard". Kendo training methodology seems irrational when you consider *shochū-geiko* (mid-summer training), and *kan-geiko* (mid-winder training) when your feet go numb with the cold. But there is an important point to it. *Keiko* is not just about improving your skills; it is also about disciplining your mind. Bolstering your mental attitude and fortitude is crucial.

I wrote the dictum "*kensokushin*" on a *shinai* bag that was created as a commemorative gift for the 25th anniversary of the Shūdōkai Kendo Club. It means, "The sword is the mind". In other words, training in kendo is to train the mind, and to train the mind is to train in kendo.

Even if you are not particularly successful in competitive kendo, persist with the basics and build a solid foundation. Like the rabbit and the tortoise, those who make the extra effort and plug away diligently will prevail in the long run. Those who don't, won't. In kendo, great talent matures later on. There is no short cut—stick to the basics and do *keiko* as much as you can. Be careful that your kendo does not devolve into tit-for-tat simple striking. Train with determination and enough willpower to become a role model in everybody's eyes.

## 15. *Keiko* alone is not enough

Do *keiko* as often as you can. The content of your *keiko* needs to be well-planned and well-executed. Regardless of your age or grade, never neglect the basics—specifically, *kirikaeshi* and *uchikomi*. They are the fundamental exercises that should always be on the menu.

Still, you might wonder if just sticking to the basics is enough. I do not believe so. Indeed, there are some people who can shine just by doing *keiko*, but I think they are a minority. You may experience steady improvement in skill, but you will hit a wall sooner or later. What makes the difference is how you climb over that wall. You need to prepare yourself for the inevitable obstacles, take the initiative and try to absorb anything that might help your kendo.

Personally, I like to run as it strengthens my lower body, and makes me feel good mentally. Furthermore, I practise breathing from my *tanden*. I only do it for ten minutes every day, but it enriches my mind, makes me settled, and by extension, it also brings my kendo up.

*run /swim / rollerblade*

Those with true ability make efforts in other areas as well. While it may seem that *keiko* is all that they are doing, most likely they are engaged in extra-curricular activities behind the scenes. Realise that *keiko* alone will not suffice—you need something extra, something to complement your *keiko*.

# CONCLUSION

I decided to pen this book to help fellow kendo practitioners. I wrote about my kendo philosophy cultivated over many years of training. I lament that due to my limited talents at writing the content may seem rather shallow. I understand that people have different values and are searching for different things. It has never been my intention to force my *keiko* methods on others, but I do hope that this humble volume is of some use to those waling the path of kendo. I wish all fellow kenshi the best of luck along their journey.

## THE KEIKO MINDSET

*If you seek a higher level of kendo, your keiko will change.*

*If your keiko changes, your lifestyle will change.*

*If your lifestyle changes, your kendo mind will change.*

*As your kendo mind changes, you will discover the way in front of you.*
*Don't look up, don't look down.*

*Be sincere and learn from both high and low.*
*Simply devote yourself to the Way.*